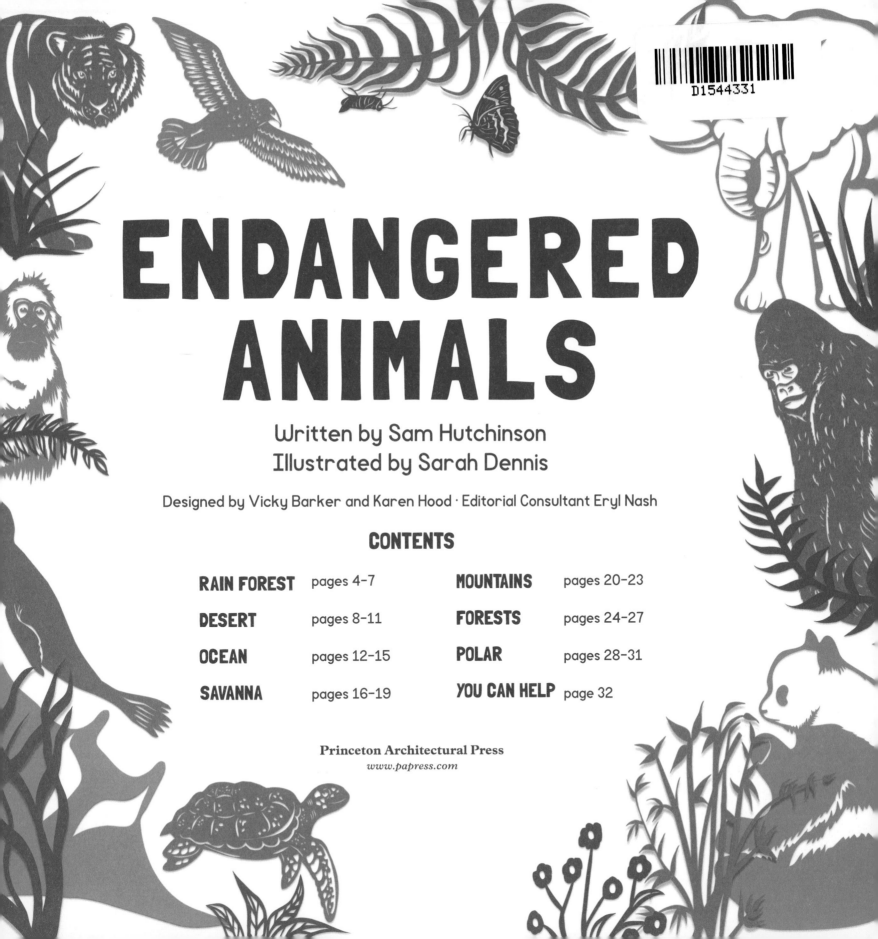

# ENDANGERED ANIMALS

Written by Sam Hutchinson
Illustrated by Sarah Dennis

Designed by Vicky Barker and Karen Hood · Editorial Consultant Eryl Nash

## CONTENTS

Princeton Architectural Press
www.papress.com

# ENDANGERED ANIMALS

The animal kingdom is a wild and colorful world. From faraway polar ice caps to humid rain forests and the deepest depths of the oceans, millions of animals thrive in every environment imaginable. And thousands more species (kinds) of animals are identified every year.

Sadly, the animals on our planet are at risk from both natural and man-made threats. Habitat loss, pollution, poaching, and changes to the world's climate are just a few of the many dangers that animals must contend with every day.

While some wild animal populations are able to adapt or recover from overhunting and habitat degradation, others have suffered in ways that cannot be reversed. This means that while some wild animal populations are stable or growing, other populations are so small—or are decreasing in number so quickly—that they are at risk of completely disappearing.

It's not just animals that suffer from these threats—other organisms, like plants and fungi, are all dependent on one another in the natural world.

**But you can help! There is still time to take action and help save the endangered animals in this book. Read through the pages, arm yourself with information, and turn to the back for more ways you can take action. Along the way, can you spot the different animals hidden in each scene?**

# Categories of Risk

One way scientists monitor which animals are under threat is by grouping them into categories based on information about a species' home range, population size, habitat, and ecology (how it relates to others and its surroundings). The IUCN (International Union for Conservation of Nature) keeps a "Red List" of at-risk species on Earth and their categories of threat. The list is a powerful tool that provides people with the information they need to make conservation decisions, and encourages people around the world to take action.

**The categories are:**

To decide whether a species faces a risk of EXTINCTION IN THE WILD, the IUCN may use surveys and research to answer questions like:

- Is the species' population smaller than a particular size?

- Has the species' population reduced at a particular rate, or is it expected to?

- Is the species' range small, fragmented, or getting smaller at a particular speed?

You'll find examples of animals from these categories in the following pages. Sometimes there are positive stories to be told: look for the green arrows that tell you that an animal population is actually increasing, and spot the animals that are classed as Least Concern because their populations are stable or thriving. There is perhaps no better news than that an animal population is recovering when conservation efforts pay off!

 a population that is increasing

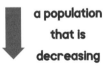 a population that is decreasing

a population that is stable

## LEAST CONCERN
a species that is widespread and abundant

## DATA DEFICIENT
not a category of threat, but means that there isn't enough available data to assess a species' risk of extinction

## NEAR THREATENED
a species that is likely to become vulnerable, endangered, or critically endangered in the near future

## VULNERABLE
a species that faces a high risk of extinction in the wild

## ENDANGERED
a species that faces a very high risk of extinction in the wild

## CRITICALLY ENDANGERED
a species that faces an extremely high risk of extinction in the wild

## EXTINCT IN THE WILD
a species that only exists in captivity or as a new population outside of its natural home range, due to extreme habitat loss

## EXTINCT
the term used when there is no reasonable doubt that the last individual of a species has died

3

# RAIN FOREST

High levels of rainfall nourish the hundreds of species of trees growing in tropical and temperate rain forests. The crowns of these trees form a canopy that is rich in plant and animal life. Many of the creatures living in or above the canopy never visit the forest floor.

The loss of "primary" (untouched) rain forest to deforestation affects the animals of this habitat in different ways. Some lose their treetop homes completely and others, living closer to or on the ground, become vulnerable to humans or struggle to compete for food and shelter.

## WIED'S MARMOSET
### Near Threatened

Limited to small areas of rain forest in eastern Brazil, these highly sociable monkeys find fruit and leaves in the middle layer of trees. Habitat loss removes their shelter and food source.

## CENTRAL AMERICAN RED BROCKET
### Data Deficient

Brocket deer rely on the dense rain forest for safety, taking shelter in small nooks. Habitat loss will almost certainly affect their survival, but they are hard to track and study.

## CAPYBARA
### Least Concern

The largest living rodent, this semi-aquatic herbivore grazes on new growth in deforested areas. Disease spreads easily between the herds, but this keeps the population size stable.

## GIANT ARMADILLO
### Vulnerable

Protected by law in many South American countries, this insectivore is still hunted for its meat and traded illegally. Deforestation threatens the remaining population.

## ALAGOAS CURASSOW
### Extinct in the Wild

Last seen in the wild in the 1980s, the only living examples of this large, black-feathered bird are with private collectors. They lost their small habitat to Brazilian sugarcane plantations.

## SPECKLE-CHESTED PICULET
### Endangered

This small, camouflaged woodpecker keeps a low profile in the rainforests of northern Peru. As the trees are removed to make way for agriculture, the population is struggling to find food.

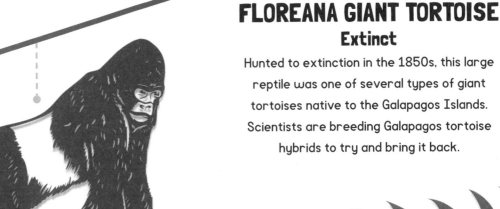

## FLOREANA GIANT TORTOISE
### Extinct

Hunted to extinction in the 1850s, this large reptile was one of several types of giant tortoises native to the Galapagos Islands. Scientists are breeding Galapagos tortoise hybrids to try and bring it back.

## GORILLA
### Critically Endangered

Deforestation opens the rain forest to poachers and disease. Primarily ground dwellers, gorillas are vulnerable to both. As they are slow to reproduce, their population is declining rapidly.

## ORANGUTAN
### Critically Endangered

Swinging from branch to vine, this solitary ape rarely leaves the treetops. Deforestation in its native Borneo and Sumatra removes any chance of this creature surviving in the wild.

Turn the page to find out how you can help.

# DEVASTATING DEFORESTATION

As human populations increase, it is important that people are aware of the impact their lives have on the natural world around them. Clearing forests for things like agriculture, construction, or timber removes the vegetation that helps produce water vapor, which can lead to reduced rainfall for thousands of miles around. Replenishing deforested areas by replanting trees, and making use of smaller areas of agricultural land by planting more efficient crops, are just two ways to begin reversing this effect.

**Can you limit your impact on the environment by using less water for a day?**

Capybara

Wied's marmoset

Gorilla

Central American red brocket

Speckle-chested piculet

Giant armadillo

Alagoas curassow

Orangutan

Floreana giant tortoise

# DESERT

True deserts are barren habitats where more water evaporates than falls and very little can grow. The rivers running through them, and the semiarid land around their edges, currently provide a lifeline for many plants and animals.

Human population growth puts pressure on fragile desert ecosystems for resources like wood, water, and agricultural land. As global temperatures rise, desert environments grow drier and hotter. Without trees for shelter, soil erodes away and sandstorms can spread arid land further into surrounding areas, destroying more biodiversity.

## ARABIAN PIPISTRELLE
### Data Deficient

These bats are very small insectivores, measuring no more than three inches. Their range is large, spanning Iran and Oman, but it is not known how many bats make up the population.

## DEMOISELLE CRANE
### Least Concern

Just under three feet in height, these tall birds are well adapted to finding food in dry conditions. Their long necks and legs—but short beaks and toes—allow them to forage, fight, and run!

## COMMON DESERT IGUANA
### Least Concern

Able to withstand very high temperatures, these omnivores thrive in a hot desert landscape and can lay two clutches of eggs per year. They rely on waxy, woody shrubs for shelter and food.

## BROWN HYENA
### Near Threatened

An opportunistic nocturnal scavenger, the brown hyena is wrongly targeted by farmers whose livestock are prey for the closely related, but not endangered, spotted hyena.

## GREAT DESERT SKINK
### Vulnerable

Road travel and invasive grasses, introduced by humans, can increase the spread of wildfires. Without shelter, this burrowing lizard becomes more vulnerable to predators.

## BROAD-CHEEKED HOPPING MOUSE
### Extinct

This rodent lost its habitat and was hunted by cats. Sadly, there are no drawings or photographs, but it came from a genus similar to the one shown here.

## DESERT BANDICOOT
### Extinct

A combination of poor fire management techniques, leading to more intense fires, and introduced predators such as cats and foxes, completely destroyed this population.

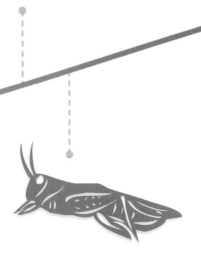

## RUGOSE SAND GRASSHOPPER
### Endangered

Already very rare, this grasshopper is an important source of food for other creatures in Lanzarote and Fuerteventura, Spain. Tourist developments destroy its habitat.

## ADDAX
### Critically Endangered

Hunted by locals for food and by tourists for sport, this large ungulate (mammal with hooves) is victim to the increased use of vehicles and sophisticated poaching techniques.

Turn the page to find out how you can help.

# TREES OF LIFE

Many deserts are already very hot places, so these habitats are particularly vulnerable to rising global temperatures. Planting trees in the land bordering deserts and reducing the amount of livestock grazing in an area can help slow down soil erosion, which may prevent deserts from spreading. Trees can also absorb a lot of carbon dioxide, which would otherwise contribute to global warming, over their lifetime.

Can you help plant new trees in your area?

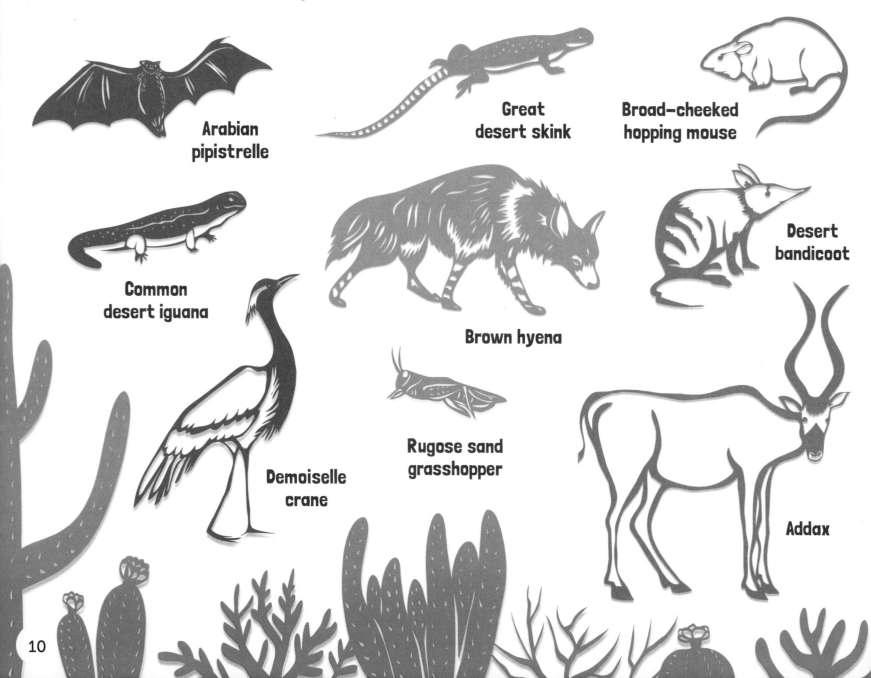

Arabian pipistrelle

Great desert skink

Broad-cheeked hopping mouse

Common desert iguana

Brown hyena

Desert bandicoot

Demoiselle crane

Rugose sand grasshopper

Addax

# OCEAN

Oceans regulate the temperature of the Earth, provide food for humans to eat, and—just like plants on land—release oxygen that humans need to breathe. Ocean currents and phytoplankton (tiny algae) work together to do these essential jobs. Phytoplankton are a source of food for many sea creatures, kick-starting the ocean food chain and sustaining nearly all marine life.

As they cover roughly 70 percent of the Earth's surface, oceans are used for international shipping and leisure travel. Tourism and pollution have a very harmful impact on the health of oceans and the creatures living in them.

## KILLER WHALE
### Data Deficient

As apex predators, killer whales are at risk from toxic chemicals building up in the food chain. Some fishermen hunt them to protect their catch, and shipping, tourism, and pollution affect their ability to find food.

## ADÉLIE PENGUIN
### Least Concern

After losing some of their habitat and food source to human activity and fishing, these flightless birds are now protected by strict regulations. Their numbers are increasing again.

## GREAT SKUA
### Least Concern

A migratory marine bird, this opportunistic feeder flies south for the winter and snaps up discarded scraps from fisheries. They are dominant seabirds and can be aggressive to humans approaching their nests.

## TIGER SHARK
### Near Threatened

Overfishing of these large, active sharks is common. Their fins, skin, liver oil, and meat are prized targets. Shark-control programs, designed to keep humans safe, and recreational fishing disrupt tiger sharks' habitats.

## BELORIBITSA
### Extinct in the Wild

Man-made dams in Russia and Central Asia have blocked access to the spawning grounds used by this fish. A few spawners survive, thanks to "fish stocking," whereby fish are raised in hatcheries before being released.

## GIANT MANTA RAY
### Vulnerable

Highly valued by some for medicinal purposes, these large, slow-moving rays are easy to catch. They are also victims of bycatch (being caught by mistake). As they do not breed before eight years of age, their population is declining.

## JAPANESE SEA LION
### Extinct

Last observed in the 1950s, these beautiful sea lions were hunted to extinction by humans who wanted their skins, whiskers, organs, and oil. Some may even have been taken for circuses.

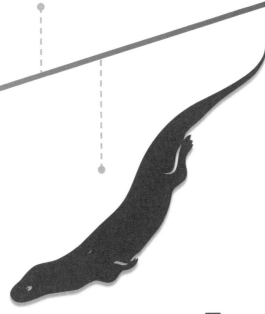

## HAWKSBILL TURTLE
### Critically Endangered

The tortoiseshell trade, now prohibited, took millions of hawksbill turtles from the seas in the last century. Threatened by poaching for their eggs and meat, habitat loss, and pollution, the population is very unlikely to recover.

## SEA OTTER
### Endangered

Making their homes close to coastal areas, sea otters are vulnerable to pollution and disease. Oil from ship spills prevents their fur from successfully insulating their bodies from the cold.

Turn the page to find out how you can help.

13

# LIFE-GIVING OCEANS

Toxic chemicals, trash, and non-recyclable plastics end up in the ocean. Plastic is not biodegradable, which means that it will never disappear. If a fish eats plastic and you eat the fish, you have just eaten plastic, too! We can help by reducing what we buy, reusing as much as possible, and if we must discard something, making sure we recycle it if possible.

**Can you try going a week without creating any plastic waste?**

Great skua

Beloribitsa

Giant manta ray

Hawksbill turtle

Adélie penguin

Tiger shark

Killer whale

Sea otter

Japanese sea lion

# SAVANNA

A savanna is a flat grassland dotted with trees, which has a dry season and a rainy season. There is just enough rain to keep the land from becoming a desert and to quench the thirst of large herds of grazing animals.

With many types of grass able to grow in one place, savannas attract commercial farmers whose livestock, together with wild animals, overgraze and turn the savanna into desert. Home to some of the largest—and most famous—herbivores on Earth, savannas also attract hunters and poachers.

## WHITE RHINOCEROS
### Near Threatened

Already quite rare, the white rhinoceros is a target for poachers who prize its horns. Surviving populations live in protected zones and rely on law enforcement for safety.

## KATANGA METAL FROG
### Data Deficient

Native to the Democratic Republic of Congo, this frog takes advantage of temporary pools to lay its frog spawn. There are similar species across sub-Saharan Africa.

## HADADA IBIS
### Least Concern

Foraging for insects in small groups during the day and roosting in large numbers together at night, these sedentary birds thrive across a large range, including savanna woodland.

## HIPPOPOTAMUS
### Vulnerable

Making their homes in and around freshwater sources, these large, amphibious herbivores are losing their habitat to humans who are diverting precious rivers and streams to nourish farmland and villages.

16

## LEOPARD
### Vulnerable

Leopards are generalists, which means they can thrive in a variety of habitats, including urban areas. As human activity increases, leopards lose a lot of their food sources. They are also a target for their patterned skin.

## SCIMITAR-HORNED ORYX
### Extinct in the Wild

Hunted to near extinction for their meat, horns, and thick skin, which was used for rope, bags, and shoes, only a small number remain. They have been released from captivity into a protected area.

## LONG-TAILED HOPPING MOUSE
### Extinct

Native to Australia, this widespread rodent was found in large numbers. Feral cats hunted them until they were all gone.

## AFRICAN ELEPHANT
### Vulnerable

Famous for their ivory tusks, these elephants have long been a target for poachers. Though they are now protected by law, their habitat is shrinking as a result of urbanization.

## BLACK RHINOCEROS
### Critically Endangered

With hooked upper lips that distinguish them from white rhinos, these gentle giants suffered at the hands of poachers in the twentieth century, but have made a comeback due to conservation efforts. There is still a lot of work to be done to stabilize their population.

Turn the page to find out how you can help.

# SOMETIMES HUMANS ARE HELPFUL

Hunters and poachers are using increasingly sophisticated techniques to secure their prey. But one of the benefits of the savanna's being home to so many famous animals, such as rhinoceroses, is that many private and government organizations help to manage protected zones that keep them safe. It is for this reason that hippopotamus and African elephant populations, for example, are gradually increasing.

Can you volunteer with an animal conservation organization near you?

Katanga metal frog

White rhinoceros

Long-tailed hopping mouse

Hadada ibis

Hippopotamus

Black rhinoceros

Leopard

African elephant

Scimitar-horned oryx

# MOUNTAINS

High up in the mountains the weather is harsh, temperatures are low, and there is very little moisture in the ground or air. There are diverse habitats that change wildly with the seasons, such as rocky cliffsides or alpine meadows, and only a few creatures are adapted to surviving in such conditions.

Since these habitats are scattered, some species are restricted to very small areas, which means mountains are very biodiverse. A small change in their habitat, such as a temperature rise or clearing of land for farming, could see some already-rare species disappear forever.

## SPOT-FRONTED SWIFT
### Data Deficient

Experts find it hard to tell different types of swifts apart, which makes it hard to keep accurate population records. Seen in conservation areas in South America, the spot-fronted swift is a bird researchers are keen to learn more about.

## STOAT
### Least Concern

This carnivorous mammal hunts other small mammals and has a huge population range around the world. It was once trapped for its fur but this practice is no longer common.

## ALPINE IBEX
### Least Concern

Scattered throughout the Alps in Europe, this ungulate lives in small groups above the tree line, where conditions are too harsh for trees to grow.

## WOODLAND GRAYLING
### Near Threatened

Brown in color and easily camouflaged against tree trunks, this butterfly inhabits semi-wild woodlands across Europe. Either an increase or a decrease in human activity can change their habitat for the worse.

## SNOW LEOPARD
### Vulnerable

Harsh mountain conditions mean there is not much suitable prey around for this cat. Livestock is an important source of food, but farmers kill snow leopards to protect their animals. Humans also hunt them for their fur and bones.

## SERBIAN STICK GRASSHOPPER
### Critically Endangered

Specific to Mount Tara in Serbia, the nymphs of this bright green insect hibernate in dead wood. When humans remove this wood from the forest, the nymphs die and cannot become adults.

## LAUGHING OWL
### Extinct

Common in New Zealand in the 1800s, this owl lost its habitat to new ways of farming and fell prey to introduced animals; it has not been seen since 1914.

## CHELMOS MOUNTAIN GRASSHOPPER
### Endangered

Found at high altitudes on Mount Chelmos, this Greek grasshopper is quickly losing its habitat to new ski slopes in the area. It does not live anywhere else so the species could disappear.

## STONE BEETLE
### Critically Endangered

This insect feeds on decomposing plants and animals. Native to a coastal volcano on Fayal Island in the Atlantic Ocean, the beetle is vulnerable to coastal erosion and will disappear, along with its habitat, unless it is protected.

Turn the page to find out how you can help.

# FUEL FOR THOUGHT

Mountains are at risk from climate change, more so than many other ecosystems on Earth. Mountain snow and glaciers are a major source of freshwater, storing it as ice in winter and releasing it during the summer to nourish plants and animals, and replenish rivers. As global warming causes glaciers to melt, the balance of life not only on the mountains but in the surrounding landscapes and rivers is affected. Burning fewer fossil fuels is one way to help prevent mountain glaciers and snow from melting, as fossil fuels release carbon dioxide into the atmosphere—a major cause of global warming.

What fuels are burned to power your home or car? Are renewable sources of energy available to you?

Spot-fronted swift

Chelmos mountain grasshopper

Serbian stick grasshopper

Woodland grayling

Alpine ibex

Stoat

Snow leopard

Laughing owl

Stone beetle

# FORESTS

Trees absorb carbon dioxide as they grow and emit it as they die. A healthy forest helps reduce carbon dioxide emissions because it has more growing trees than dying trees. These trees also provide a home to 80 percent of the world's terrestrial plant and animal life.

As forests are cleared for grazing livestock and new towns and cities, more carbon dioxide remains in the atmosphere, contributing to global warming. Increased contact with humans also puts plants and animals in forests at risk. Changes in their ecosystems lead to insect outbreaks, wildfires, destructive storms, diseases, and the arrival of invasive species from other environments.

## EUROPEAN RABBIT
### Near Threatened

Foraging in small groups, this rabbit damages crops. Farmers introduced a South American virus to control the population but it worked too well, killing nine in every ten rabbits.

## LACTARIUS CORDOVAENSIS
### Data Deficient

Only recorded in Alaska, this mushroom is an example of our planet's biodiversity that can easily be lost if it is not protected.

## PINE MARTEN
### Least Concern

Pine martens eat a wide range of food, from rodents to mushrooms and berries. They are able to cope well with changes to their usual habitat.

## GIANT PANDA
### Vulnerable

About a third of the panda's native bamboo forests have been lost to growing towns and cities. Pandas have been pushed higher up into the mountains, limiting their ability to travel to different areas of the forest for food.

# TIGER
## Endangered

Highly prized for their skin, meat, and bones, tigers are most at risk from poachers. Sharing their tropical Asian habitat with large and growing human populations means they must compete for food and are killed by farmers protecting livestock.

# CHINESE PANGOLIN
## Critically Engangered

A ground-dwelling creature, the Chinese pangolin is unable to evade hunters who want to catch it and sell its meat and scales. The scales are used for medicine.

# AUROCH
## Extinct

Last seen in Poland in 1627, this large herbivore preferred swampy forests. Humans domesticated aurochs as cattle and the wild animals died out.

# FRENCH STONE GRASSHOPPER
## Endangered

Preferring dry, open habitats, this flightless grasshopper is actually a victim of humans trying to help. Planting trees in open areas to create new forests depletes its habitat.

# CALIFORNIA CONDOR
## Critically Endangered

The population of this large scavenger dropped drastically in the twentieth century because of lead poisoning. The small carcasses they find and eat often contain lead bullets.

Turn the page to find out how you can help.

# NEW TO THE NEIGHBORHOOD

Forest animals are particularly vulnerable to new, non-native species of animals or plants, often introduced by humans in nearby towns and cities. Food webs are complicated systems of overlapping food chains and are very delicate, so removing or adding just one creature can affect all the other living things in the chain. Education goes a long way toward preventing this from happening, by teaching people about the importance of protecting the local environment from invasive species.

Are there any non-native plants causing damage near where you live? Can you volunteer with a local preserve or native plant society to learn more about local ecology?

Pine marten

Tiger

California condor

Lactarius cordovaensis

Chinese pangolin

Giant panda

European rabbit

French stone grasshopper

Auroch

# POLAR

Food chains in the polar regions are limited because there are not many creatures that can survive the cold temperatures. Much of the plant and animal life in these regions centers around the coming and going of the sea ice, which builds up in the colder months and melts in the warmer months.

Climate change is reducing the buildup of sea ice each winter, meaning the sea ice melts earlier in the spring. The animals that rely on the sea ice for food, hunting, shelter, or protection then struggle to survive.

## HIGH ARCTIC BUMBLEBEE
### Data Deficient

This bee relies on stealing other bees' hives. As global warming reduces the winter snow, the summer months are drier. This means fewer flowers, fewer bees and so, no hives to steal.

## COMMON COOT
### Least Concern

Protected in some parts of the world, while hunted or losing habitats in others, the populations of this bird are widespread. The polar population is migratory.

## ANTARCTIC KRILL
### Least Concern

Widespread in the Southern Ocean, this small crustacean lives in swarms and its population is measured in metric tons. Meaning "whale food" in Norwegian, krill is essential to the polar food web.

## EMPEROR PENGUIN
### Near Threatened

Emperor penguins nest on the thick sea ice that forms along the coast of Antarctica in the winter months. Climate change is making the sea ice less regular and reliable, preventing successful breeding.

## POLAR BEAR
### Vulnerable

After sheltering from the winter, polar bears emerge in desperate need of nutrition. They hunt for seals on the sea ice, but as climate change reduces the amount of ice, they are increasingly unable to find food.

## ARCTIC BLUE WHALE
### Critically Endangered

The largest animal ever recorded, the blue whale feeds on krill. Having been hunted almost to extinction in the 1900s, it is now protected and the population is slowly growing.

## GREAT AUK
### Extinct

Not seen since 1852, this penguin-like bird lived across the North Atlantic. It was hunted to extinction for its feathers, meat, fat, and oil.

## ATLANTIC PETREL
### Endangered

This seabird wanders the ocean, returning to the remote Gough Island in the South Atlantic to lay its eggs in June. Mice, introduced by humans, are attacking these seabirds' chicks and destroying the population.

## SOUTHERN BLUEFIN TUNA
### Critically Endangered

This type of tuna has been extensively overfished. It is now protected by a "quota," or a maximum amount that can be fished, but evidence suggests the quota is being broken. The population is decreasing and not recovering.

Turn the page to find out how you can help.

# WARMING UP TO DISEASE

Polar bears are much less likely than other types of bears to catch diseases or have parasites. This is because the extreme cold weather in the polar regions makes it hard for diseases and parasites to survive. However, as global temperatures rise, polar bears and other animals—already in a weakened state due to lack of food and nutrition—are more likely to catch or spread diseases. Eating less meat is one way to help reduce carbon emissions, and it will help lessen the effect of climate change on these regions.

Can you try eating less meat or going meat-free for one day?

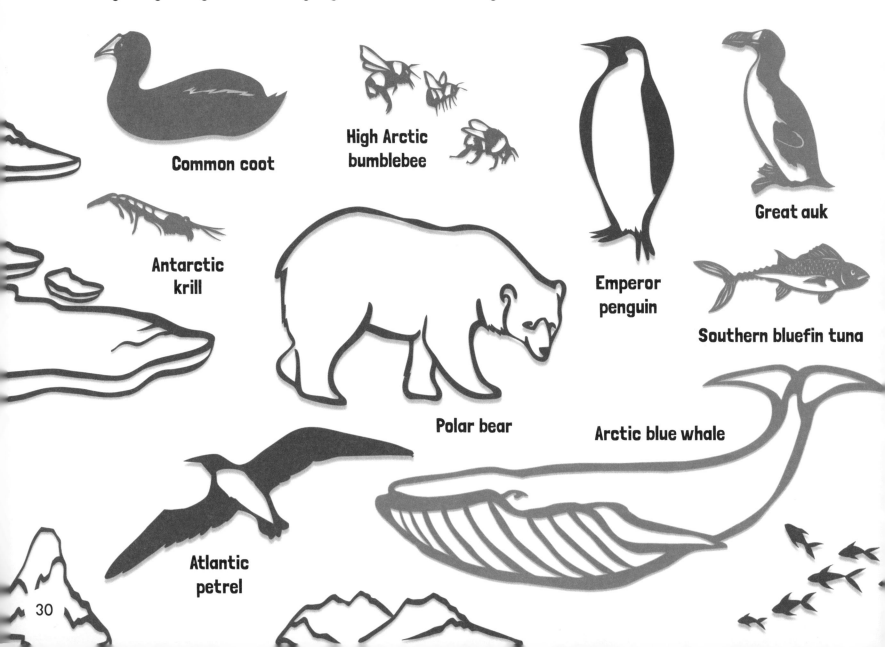

Common coot

High Arctic bumblebee

Great auk

Antarctic krill

Emperor penguin

Southern bluefin tuna

Polar bear

Arctic blue whale

Atlantic petrel

# YOU CAN HELP

Small changes can make a big difference to the world around us. Here are some more ways you can improve the future of the endangered animals in this book:

Avoid buying or using products that use a lot of plastic packaging, as not all plastic can be easily recycled.

Turn off electronic devices when you're not using them to save energy that relies on the burning of fossil fuels.

Instead of jumping in a car, try to walk, cycle, and use public transportation as much as possible to reduce how much carbon dioxide you contribute to the atmosphere.

Recycle as much as you can—from plastic to cardboard and aluminum—and always use recycling bins when you're out and about.

Education is power: read and learn as much as you can about climate change and how to help the environment. The more you know, the better decisions you can make on a daily basis, and the more you can teach others around you.

Published by Princeton Architectural Press, 202 Warren Street, Hudson, New York, 12534
Text and illustrations © b small publishing ltd. 2020   1 2 3 4 5 6 7 8 9 10   All rights reserved.
Princeton Architectural Press edition first published in arrangement with b small publishing ltd. in 2020
No part of this publication may be reproduced, stored in a retrieval system, or transmitted in any form or by any means (including electronic, mechanical, photocopying, recording or otherwise) without the prior permission from b small publishing.
Production: Madeleine Ehm   Publisher: Sam Hutchinson   Editorial: Eryl Nash   Printed in China by WKT Co. Ltd.
Library of Congress Cataloging-in-Publication Data is available upon request.